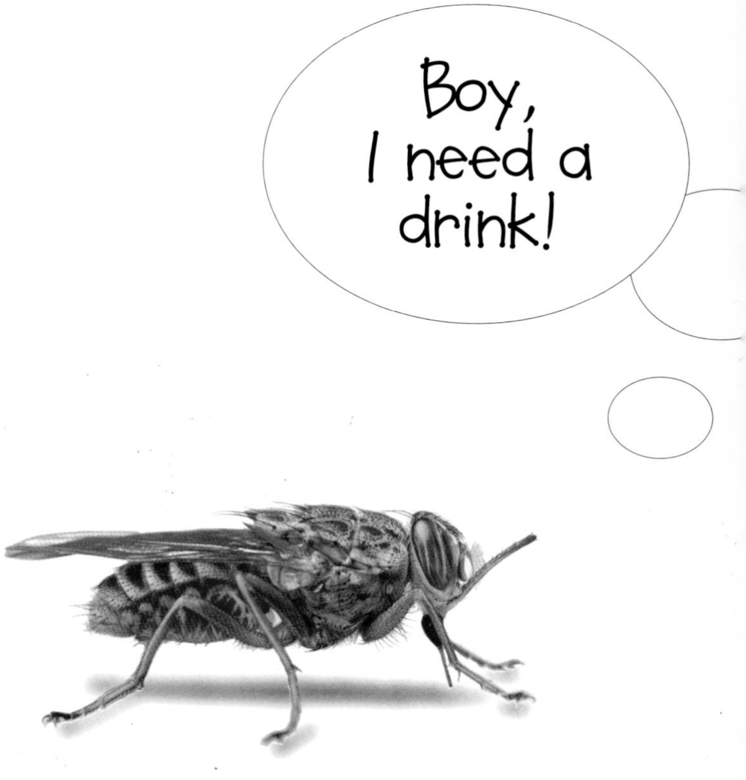
Boy,
I need a
drink!

written by **trevor day**

edited by **dugald steer**

designed by **mike jolley**

Simon & Schuster Books for Young Readers
An imprint of Simon & Schuster Children's Publishing Division
1230 Avenue of the Americas, New York, New York 10020

Text and design copyright © 2000 by the Templar Company plc
Photographs copyright © 2000 by Bruce Coleman Collection, FPG/Robert Harding Picture Library, Natural History Photographic Agency, Oxford Scientific Films, Planet Earth Pictures, Science Photo Library, and individual copyright holders

Devised and produced by the Templar Company plc, Pippbrook Mill, Dorking, Surrey, RH4 1JE, UK

SIMON & SCHUSTER CHILDREN'S BOOKS FOR YOUNG READERS
is a trademark of Simon & Schuster.

ISBN 0-689-83416-0

Library of Congress Catalog Card Number: 99-47355
Printed in Hong Kong
1 2 3 4 5 6 7 8 9 10

front cover: top: Science Photo Library (SPL), bottom, from left: Andrew Syred/SPL, Claude Nuridsany & Marie Perennou/SPL, David Scharf/SPL; spine: Andrew Syred/SPL; back cover, top left: Dennis Hallinan/Robert Harding Picture Library (RHPL), top right: Dr Jeremy Burgess/SPL, bottom right: CNRI/SPL, bottom left: Jane Burton/Bruce Coleman Collection (BCC); page 3: Kim Taylor/BCC; page 5: Andrew Syred/SPL; pages 6-7: left to right: Breck P Kent/Oxford Scientific Films (OSF), M P L Fogden/BCC, Sinclair Stammers/SPL, Nile Root/Custom Medical Stock Photo/SPL, Dennis Hallinan/RHPL; pages 8-9: left: David Scharf/SPL, under flap, left and inset: Manfred Kage/SPL, top right: Claude Nuridsany & Marie Perennou/SPL, center right: London School of Hygiene/SPL, bottom right: Eye of Science/SPL; pages 10-11: left: Joe McDonald/ BCC, top center: Ken Lucas/PEP, center and under flap: Joe McDonald/BCC, under flap top right: Brian Kenney/Planet Earth Pictures (PEP), bottom right: Gunter Ziezler/BCC; pages 12-13: left and on flap: Andrew Syred/SPL, under flap left background: Geoff Kidd/OSF, bottom left: Andrew Syred/SPL, right, top to bottom: Breck P Kent/OSF, David Fox/OSF, Stephen Dalton/NHPA, Joe & Carol McDonald/OSF; pages 14-15: left: Tony Allen/OSF under flap, right: Staffan Widstrand/BCC, top: Green Films/OSF, bottom right: Max Gibbs/OSF, center left: Dave Roberts/SPL; pages 16-17: left: Mary Clay/PEP, inset: Breck P Kent/OSF, under flap top left: Claude Nuridsany & Marie Perennou/SPL, bottom left: Fritz Prenzel/BCC, right: Michael McCoy/BCC, bottom right: Mantis Wildlife Films/OSF; pages 18-19: left: Pacific Stock/BCC, on flap: Andrew Mounter/PEP, under flap left: Gary Bell/PEP, center: Karen Gowlett-Holmes/OSF, top: Pacific Stock/BCC, top right: Chris Prior/PEP, bottom right: Jane Burton/BCC; pages 20-21: left: M P L Fogden/BCC, center: Michael Fogden/OSF, on flap and bottom left under flap: Dr Morley Read/SPL, under flap top right: Juan M Renjito/OSF, bottom left: Kathie Atkinson /OSF; pages 22-23: center: Dr Jeremy Burgess/SPL, under flap top left: Andrew Syred/SPL, center: Dr Jeremy Burgess/SPL, top right: Nile Root/ Custom Medical Stock Photo/SPL, center right: Dr Frieder Sauer/OSF, bottom right: Scott Camazine/OSF; pages 24-25: center: Jane Burton/BCC, under flap bottom left: John Visser/BCC, top right: Brian Kenney/PEP, bottom right: Andre Bartschi/PEP; pages 26-27: center: David Scharf/SPL, under flap top left: London Scientific Films/OSF, top center: Dr Morley Read/SPL, on right: CNRI/SPL, bottom center: Martin Dohrn/SPL; pages 28-29: bottom left: Steve Turner/OSF, top left: Brian Kenney/PEP, top right: Erwin & Peggy Bauer/BCC, bottom right: Hans Reinhard/BCC, bottom center: David B Fleetham/BCC, under flap left: Claude Nuridsany & Marie Perennou/SPL, top right: Stephen Dalton/OSF, center right: Kim Taylor/BCC, bottom right: Niall Benvie/OSF; pages 30-31: center: Philip Sharpe/OSF, counterclockwise from top center: Geoff Dore/BCC, Stephen J Krasemann/BCC, Daniel Heuclin/NHPA, Nigel Downer/PEP, Alan Stillwell/BCC, Stephen J Krasemann/BCC, Sinclair Stammers/SPL, M P L Fogden/BCC, under flap: Stephen J Krasemann/BCC; page 32: Kim Taylor/BCC

Real-life monsters, **up close**

YOUCH!
it
bites!

watch your step!

If you go down to the woods today, you're sure of a scary surprise. Because the woods, and many other places, are crawling with all sorts of horrible little plants and creatures. If you get in their way they might bite, prick, or sting you. Some of them can even kill. And many of them are much more dangerous to you than any kind of big creature you might be frightened of. Let **Youch!** be your guide to some of nature's real-life monsters, up

youch!

close!

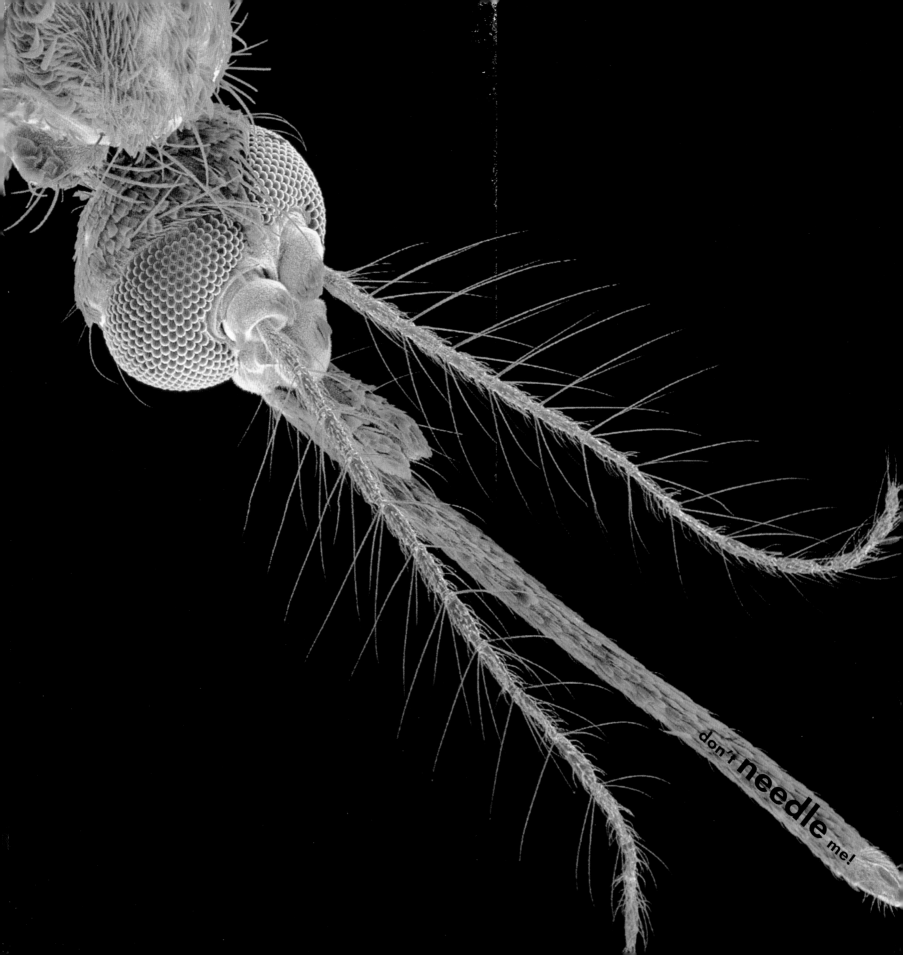

don't needle me!

This creature delivers a deadly package that kills more than one million people every year.

It may have its sights set on you. If so, it can really get under your skin. Often more annoying than deadly, you just want it to

buzz off...

What is this creature, and why is it sometimes so dangerous? Lift the flap to find out.

it started

with a

hiss!

bite fright

Despite warnings, hundreds of thousands of people are bitten by creatures like these each year. Thirty to forty thousand die as a result. Though two of the species here do not pose a threat to humans, the other has the **power to kill!**

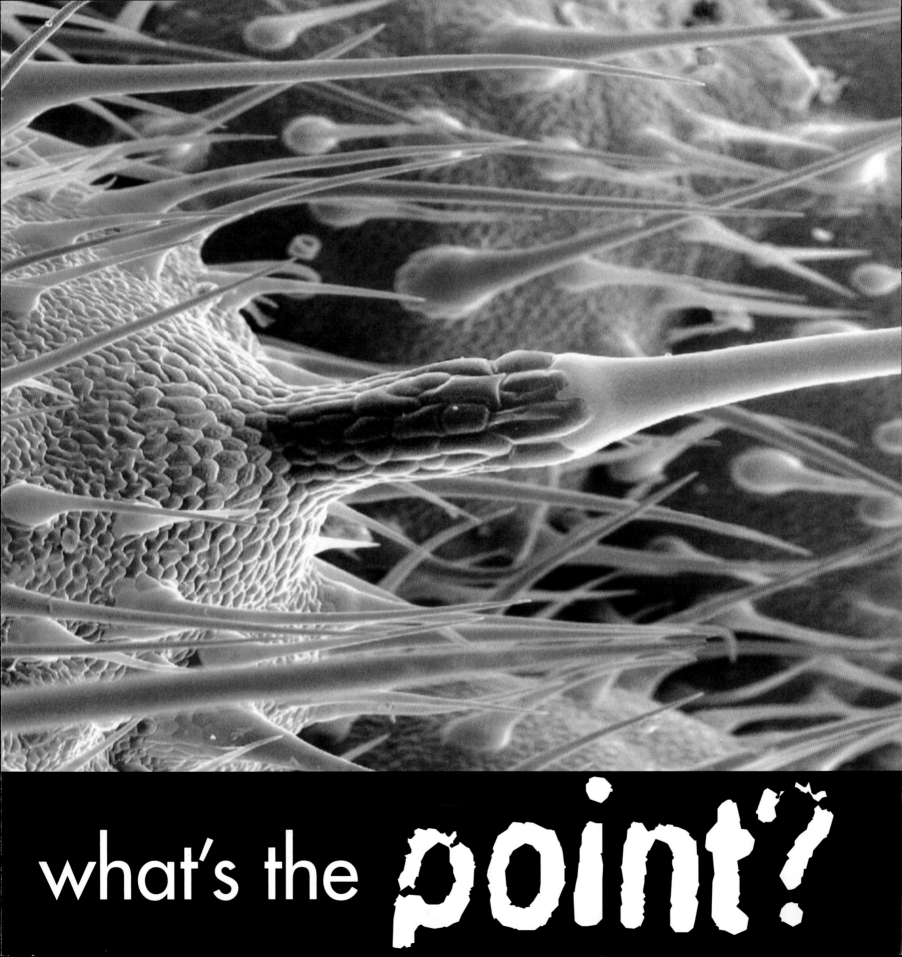

what's the **point?**

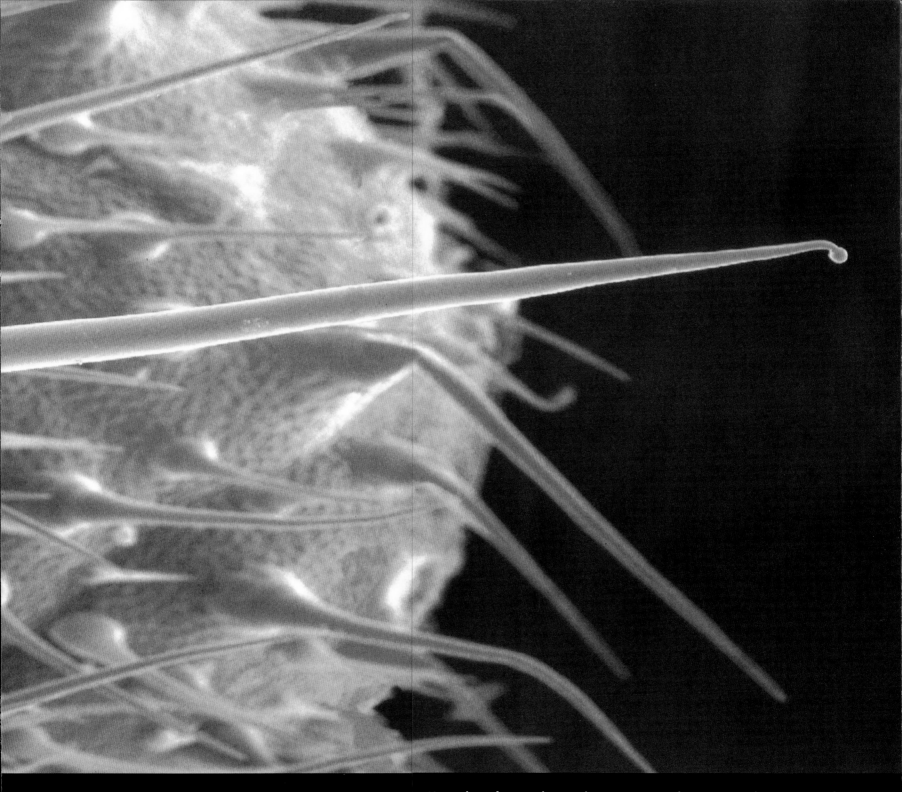

Hard tipped and razor sharp, these spines

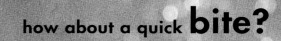

how about a quick **bite?**

friend?

Just when you thought it was **safe** to go for a swim, it's lunchtime down at the creek. And guess **who's** on the menu?

One of these creatures is a **killer.**

small and scary?

big and hairy?

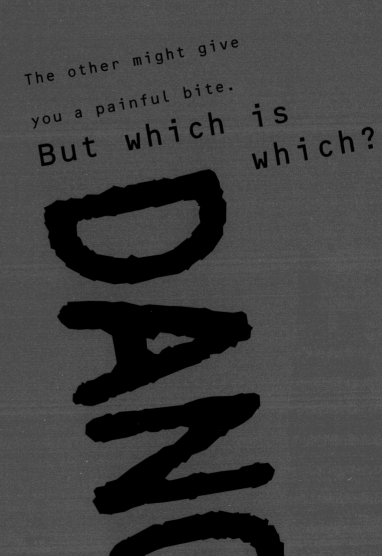

The other might give you a painful bite. But which is which?

DANGER!

Some kind of UFO?

An extraterrestrial on the move?

an alien thing?

You are experiencing **a close encounter** of the jiggly kind. This creature may seem like a soft touch, but those tentacles hide deadly weapons. So, which creature do they belong to?

pretty...

Look at these hoppy little fellows. Don't they look pretty? Perhaps if you were a princess you might kiss one, and hope he turned into a handsome prince. I wouldn't kiss one if I were you. Not unless you want to

croak!

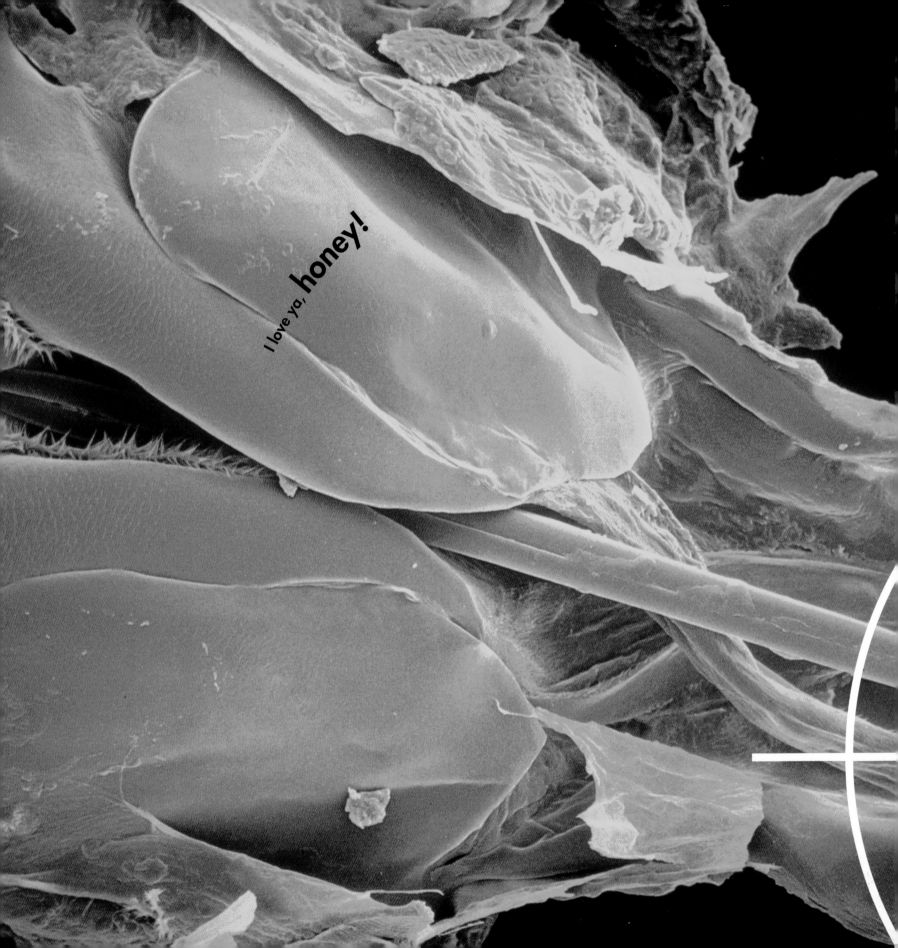

I love ya, **honey!**

beware!

This needle may be small, but it can be deadly. You may have met its owner on a sunny day. In fact, this animal **kills** thousands of people each year. So, which creature does this weapon belong to? Is your head **buzzing** with ideas?

little **nipper?**

heads, I win!

Here's a little fellow you might not want to meet in the dark. You'd find it difficult to see him at night. So hopefully, he'd avoid you. Delicate hairs on his legs and pincers would sense your footsteps. He'd try to get out of your way, but if he couldn't he'd defend himself. **Which end is more deadly? Head or tail?**

I've got you **under my skin!**

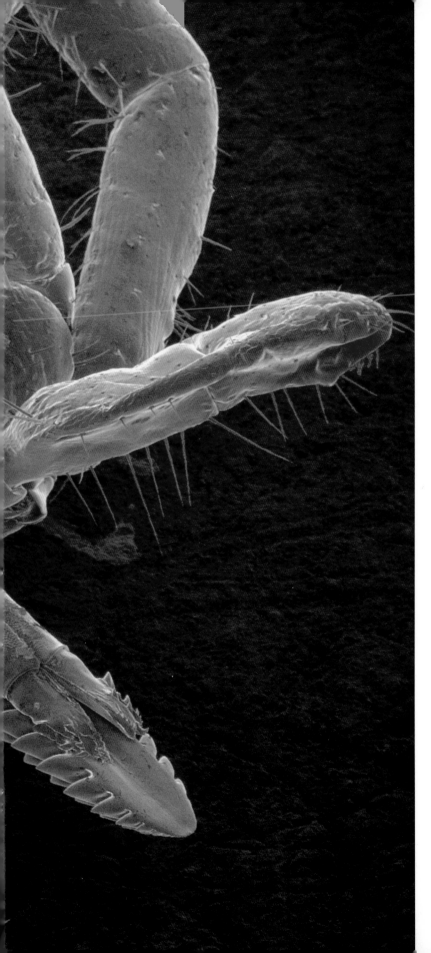

take a bite

Does this fellow look a bit scary? Is he **bugging** you? He won't bore you to death, but he can be a real pain. And there are hordes of other little creatures just like him. Who could he be? Wait a tick before lifting the flap to find out....

king of the beasts?

1

what big

2 **3** in the swim?

the real King Kong?

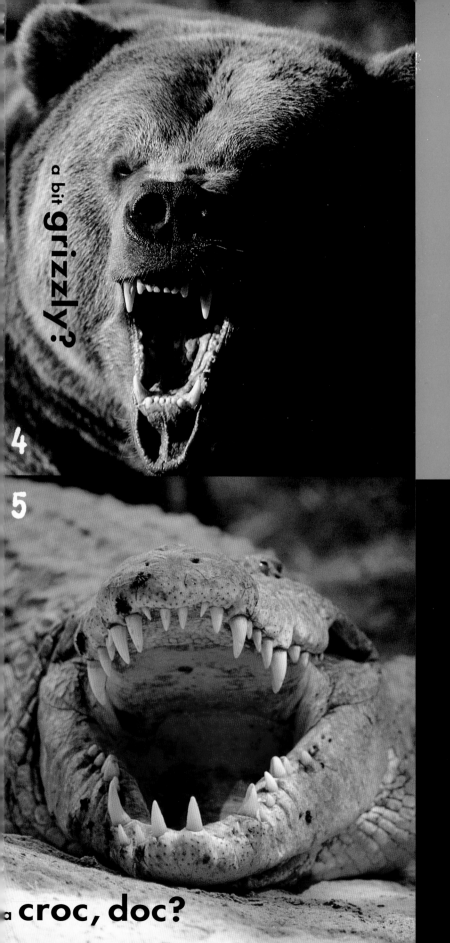

a bit **grizzly?**

a **croc, doc?**

Throughout this book we have seen some of the small creatures that can be dangerous to humans. But which one do you really not want to meet on a dark night? Could it be one of these fearsome beasts? **Just who is the number one killer?**

teeth
you have!

Would any of these animals **chew on you?**

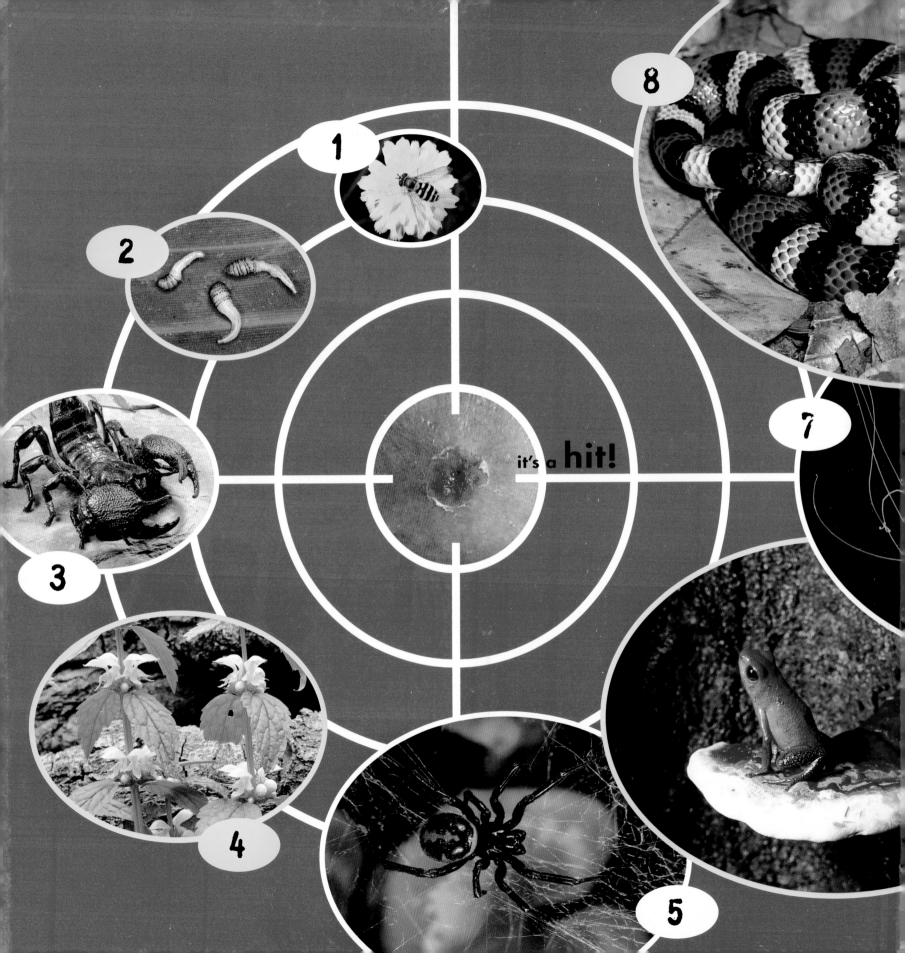

it's a **hit!**

who dunit

?

Here is an ugly little wound, and eight suspects. Trouble is, four of them are completely harmless, and three of the nasty ones are innocent.

Who is the perp?